THE
PEOPLE'S
PALACE

THE
PEOPLE'S
PALACE

THE STORY OF THE CHICAGO CULTURAL CENTER

INTRODUCTION BY M.W. NEWMAN   TEXT BY NANCY SEEGER

RESEARCH COMPILED AND EDITED BY ROLF ACHILLES

Designed and typeset
in Monotype Grotesque
and Filosofia
by studio blue, Chicago

Printed by The Stinehour
Press, Lunenburg, Vermont

Cover photo:
Exterior of the library from
South (1897)

ISBN 0-938903-25-X

City of Chicago
Richard M. Daley, Mayor

Department of Cultural Affairs
Lois Weisberg, Commissioner

Chicago Cultural Center
78 E. Washington Street
Chicago, IL 60602
312 744 6630
www.ci.chi.il.us/Tour/
CulturalCenter/

PHILIP MORRIS COMPANIES INC.
PHILIP MORRIS U.S.A. · KRAFT FOODS, INC
MILLER BREWING COMPANY

Acknowledgments.

This publication was supported in part by grants from Philip Morris Companies, Inc., the Graham Foundation for Advanced Studies in the Fine Arts and the Otto W. Lehmann Foundation.

We would like to thank the following individuals without whose help, input, information and memories this history of the Chicago Cultural Center could not have been possible:	Kathleen Cummings	Janet Carl Smith
	Nicole Cioper	Tim Samuelson
	Kristina Findlay	Commissioner
	Denise King	Lois Weisberg
	Gregory K. Knight	Valentine Judge,
	James Y. Law	Project Manager

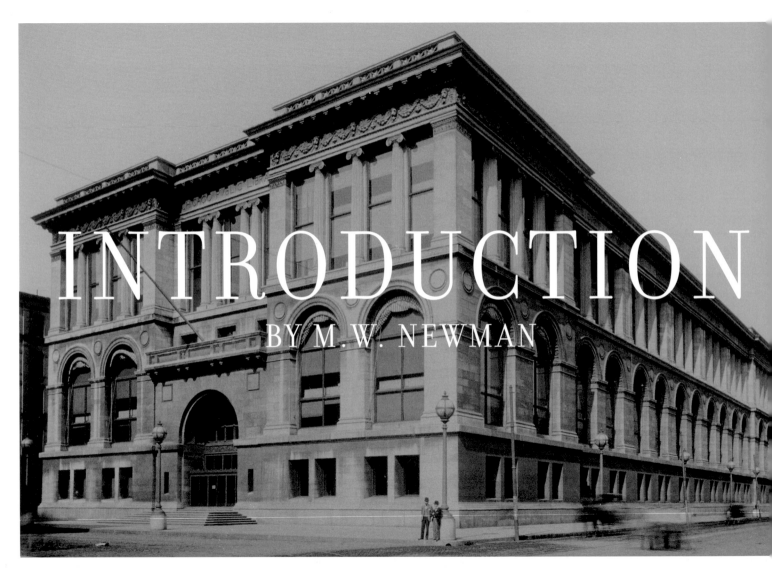

INTRODUCTION

BY M.W. NEWMAN

Perhaps you've seen those mad photos of downtown Chicago in the 1890s – a swollen instant city. The tale is preserved in those old glass-negative pictures of city streets – State and Madison, Randolph and Dearborn. There in the core of the Loop, every inch seemed to be consumed by streetcars and vans and carts and buggies and early horseless carriages and stores and business houses and people – everywhere.

Jane Addams knocked on doors at City Hall to try to get the garbage picked up on the immigrant West Side. Her name is hallowed now as Chicago's Nobel-laureate friend of the poor. Architect Frank Lloyd Wright was on those Loop streets and so were merchant princes A. Montgomery Ward and city planner Daniel Burnham ("Make no little plans," he taught) and defense lawyer Clarence Darrow and philosopher John Dewey and symphony conductor Theodore Thomas and others.

Chicago had heaved itself up from mud and flames in less than a lifetime. Railroads and mail-order houses made it go. So did grain trading and factories, slaughterhouses and skyscrapers – and slums and strikes and bloody class strife in the streets.

"The only great city," said its acerbic novelist, Henry B. Fuller, "to which all its citizens have come for the avowed purpose of making money." But those who did wanted the world to know the city had grown up. With a grand flourish, the raw city evolved a dreamlike expression of itself in the World's Columbian Exposition of 1893, only 22 years after its devastating Great Fire.

The shimmering white World's Fair buildings, a City Beautiful in plaster, were built for a single summer of dazzlement. With another grand sweep, the city built the Chicago Public Library, now the Chicago Cultural Center whose 100 years of achievement we celebrate in this book. Like the fair buildings, the library was a palace — a people's palace.

"Every city has its moment when it reaches maturity," says Donald L. Miller, an eminent historian of Chicago at Lafayette College in Pennsylvania. "Florence in the Renaissance period had it. Chicago had it."

As we look around today, we see that we still "have it." Chicago, to be sure, has been a throwaway city that has sacrificed big pieces of itself over the years. Some of the treasures we have kept are depicted in the architectural landmark gallery of the Chicago Cultural Center. Its own classical façade and jeweled salons were ordered up by commissioners who knew exactly what they wanted the building to say about itself and its city.

Ample work space, and the ornate splendor of the
library's interior were just a few of the features that drew
Chicagoans to its reading rooms.

They got what they ordered: a palace coated in massive blocks of limestone and granite, with columns and deep arches as decorative as the ones at the world's fair. But this palace also had immense windows to let in as much light for users as possible. And the library board announced significantly, "it should convey to the beholder that it is an enduring monument, worthy of a great and public-spirited city." It was made for everyone and welcomes everyone.

What's more, it went up on public ground worth a fortune if put to commercial purpose. Go-getter Chicago was serving notice that it was knitting itself into world culture and stating its claims in monumental, if traditional, architecture. Beauty was not to be the monopoly of the gifted few. In this building, at any rate, beauty was to be everyone's democratic right.

Inside, the palace emerged creamy, even lush, coated with marble, inlaid with swirling mosaics under art-glass domes. Expert hands built it all. They laid on opulent colors and ornamentation in the finest materials.

You want to touch. The building reaches out. And because it was built to endure, it looks as fresh-minted as ever today — a handsomely restored and maintained monument of cultural pride.

Above all, it's a splendid survivor. It stands today, cherished and in full use. Except for the addition of modern utility systems and interior corridors, it remains barely changed from its original appearance.

This grande dame of a building served as a central library for more than 70 years. Over time it became too small, too congested. It wasn't outdated, merely outgrown. But that was enough to put it in peril.

In the early 1970s the City of Chicago stepped in to save and rework it into a civic center of the living arts. Merging yesterday and today, the palace now showcases the rich talent springing from Chicago neighborhoods.

Its full-bodied elegance is enchanting, of course, in our spartan age of flat-chested architecture. But its role is even more significant. The building stands on land across Michigan Avenue from Grant Park, that sweep of public greenery at the city's edge dedicated to remain "forever open, clear, and free."

The Chicago Cultural Center works as today's version of the majestic Golden Door designed by architect Louis Sullivan at the 1893 fair. The building boasts two beckoning entrances: Roman-styled on Washington Street and Greek-influenced on Randolph Street. We enter at Washington Street into a hall of precious white marble glinting with mosaics and bits of colored glass — millions of pieces, seemingly. A grand staircase angles upward for four stories to a coffered ceiling with Tiffany chandeliers.

Light from tall windows streams onto inlaid walls, stairwells, archways. If we are lucky, we hear orchestral music drifting from the third-floor Preston Bradley Hall, once the library's receiving room. Now the space serves as a concert hall and civic gathering place caked and creamed in swirls of mosaics and marble under a 38-foot-wide Tiffany dome.

Music once performed for European grandees in palaces is now played in this palace. Through arched windows, we see a city backdrop of parks and lake and skyscrapers. As we proceed through the building we see that every room is a period piece of virtuoso design and Victorian grandeur. And yet the building is no mere replay of a nostalgic past. It came out of its time, solidly engineered, and using what was then advanced manufacturing.

Frank Lloyd Wright, it is true, complained that the exterior design amounted to a forced marriage of Ionic columns atop arched windows. The three-foot-thick supporting walls were a throwback at a time when Chicago was perfecting steely modern architecture on every other street in the Loop. The building, like the city itself, has its contradictions. "Do I contradict myself?" Walt Whitman once wrote. "Very well then I contradict myself. (I am large, I contain multitudes.)"

On any day the multitudes come to the building's halls and exhibit spaces, its theatres and dance studio, its salons and broadcast museum, gift shop and visitor information center. The palace meets the needs of today, but with more sheer delight than we permit ourselves in the buildings of our time. How lucky we are to have this palace in a city that knows how to use it. The Chicago Cultural Center is an essential piece of a larger cultural community, much of it integrated into the city rather than standing aloof from it. It shows how far the city has come from the days when it was striving to prove that it was more than a pigsticker town.

Even more important, the city itself is a cultural center, a creative crucible. Its neighborhoods generate dreamers: writers, painters, sculptors, photographers, musicians, architects, dancers, scholars. Many are getting their chance to be seen and heard in the Chicago Cultural Center.

Chicago is hardly a finished city. It contradicts itself in a thousand ways. But cities are always unfinished. The Chicago Cultural Center is a vital part of a living city forever finding itself.

THE CHICAGO
CULTURAL
CENTER WELCOMES YOU...

Today, when you walk into the Chicago Cultural Center, you enter a world of culture that is uniquely Chicago. It is a magical tour, whether you go in through the gleaming Carrara marble and Tiffany glass Washington Street side or the more boisterously crowded, yet tranquil Randolph Street side. Somewhere in this marvelous building, at any hour of the day and into the night, people of all definitions, from near and far, are enjoying the multitude of exciting free events sponsored by the Chicago Department of Cultural Affairs.

This is a People's Palace – a celebration of the arts, education, Chicago, and the world. Constructed over 100 years ago as the Chicago Public Library and a Civil War memorial, the Chicago Cultural Center reflects the best of Chicago.

Chicago... in the beginning.

History books are filled with stories about old Chicago – DuSable's Trading Post. Battles at Fort Dearborn. The Great Fire of Chicago. The World's Columbian Exposition. These and many other historic events set the stage for Chicago today, one of the most beautiful and dynamic cities in the world... and Chicago tomorrow.

CHICAGO WAS INCORPORATED IN 1837. THIRTY-THREE YEARS
LATER, IN OCTOBER 1871,

FIRE

RAGED THROUGH THE CITY'S CORE, BURNING FOUR SQUARE MILES,
KILLING 250 PEOPLE, LEAVING 100,000 PEOPLE HOMELESS, AND

DESTROYING 18,000 BUILDINGS.

CHICAGO WAS FIRE-SWEPT AND ALMOST TOTALLY DESTROYED.

In the spirit of dedication and determination so representative of its citizens, the city was soon rebuilt. A year after the fire, new buildings appeared every day. By 1875, many busy streets were lined with tall marble buildings, some an unimaginable nine stories high, made possible by the recently invented elevator. The sounds of construction were everywhere. Crossroad of the nation's rail lines and center for meatpacking, as well as a major harbor for ships on the Great Lakes, Chicago grew and grew. Even in this rugged environment, citizens showed an appreciation for culture and learning.

A public library for Chicago.

The first library in Chicago dates back to 1834 when the Chicago Lyceum maintained a circulating library of 300 volumes for its members. The Lyceum's popularity faded and in 1841 some of its members formed a new cultural center, the Young Men's Association. The Association had a public reading room with a collection of 30,000 books, all of which were destroyed in the fire of 1871.

Soon after the fire, Chicagoans received about 8,000 books from distinguished British authors and statesmen who wanted to help replace those that were destroyed. Many volumes were autographed by their donors, including Queen Victoria, John Stuart Mill, Charles Darwin, Robert Browning, John Ruskin and Alfred Lord Tennyson. With these books as the base of the collection, Chicago's leaders established the Chicago Public Library in April 1872.

To aid in the storage and retrieval of the library's collection, the
rooms containing the book stacks featured glass floors
to allow natural light to pass through from one level to another.

The Library Board arranged for the collection to be housed in an old water tank. For many years following, the library occupied various temporary spaces while Board members looked for a permanent site. By 1874, the collection was available for circulation without charge to all Chicagoans, and two years later it had 120,000 volumes! By 1891, Chicago boasted the largest library system in the country. William Frederick Poole, the city's distinguished librarian and a nationally recognized scholar, is credited for much of the library's success in that era.

Following the Great Fire, the library's collection was housed in a former water tank, where the city's first public reading room opened in January 1872.

FINALLY, THE LIBRARY BOARD SELECTED

DEARBORN

PARK

AS A PERMANENT SITE AND IN 1893 THE CHICAGO CITY COUNCIL

GRANTED THE
REQUIRED APPROVAL.

The library board secured Dearborn Park as the future site of the Public Library. Throughout its history, the park was the site of political rallies where notable figures including Abraham Lincoln, Ulysses S. Grant, and Stephen Douglas spoke.

1893:
Chicago presents the World's
Columbian Exposition.

As planning for the library continued, Chicagoans were presenting their beautiful, vigorous and prosperous city to the more than one million people who came to the famous World's Columbian Exposition in 1893. The main buildings were designed in a neo-classical style. The Museum of Science and Industry is the only structure remaining from the Fair. The success of the World's Fair convinced many city leaders that Chicago could compete with any major American or European city. It also inspired visionaries like Daniel Burnham, who some years later presented the city with his brilliant 1909 Plan of Chicago.

World's Columbian Exposition, 1893

A dual-purpose building.

The Library Board envisioned a splendid building that would enrich Chicago's cultural and intellectual life. However, before plans could be prepared, a conflict arose over control of Dearborn Park because the state legislature had given the north quarter of the park to an American Civil War veterans organization called the Soldier's Home. An agreement was finally signed in 1891 that specified two distinct purposes for the building: that it be the Chicago Public Library as well as a Grand Army of the Republic Memorial Hall dedicated to Northern soldiers who fought in the Civil War.

In order to finance the structure, an unusual method of funding was implemented. Instead of seeking philanthropic support from a privileged group, as was often done for such projects, the City Council levied a 1% tax on its citizens. That way it could be said that the library truly belonged to the people of Chicago.

Rowena Fry captured Assembly Hall of the Grand Army of the Republic in this painting during the 1930s.

The architects' vision.

Once financing was established, the Library Board requested bids from architectural firms throughout the nation. The Instructions to Architects specified that the new library "convey to the beholder the idea that the building would be an enduring monument worthy of a great and public spirited city."

In February, 1892, the Boston firm of Shepley Rutan and Coolidge (known today as Shepley Bulfinch Richardson and Abbott) was awarded the contract to design the library. These three young architects were the successors to the office of Henry Hobson Richardson, one of America's foremost nineteenth-century architectural firms. Talented and popular, they had just completed the original building of The Art Institute of Chicago.

The architects' final concept for the library was a neo-classical building that included powerful Greek columns and sturdy Roman arches. Adhering to the Board's rigid and detailed specifications for the structure, Shepley Rutan and Coolidge's design showed a unified exterior with an interior that served the purposes of a library and a war memorial.

1892 groundbreaking.

With great fanfare and excitement, a groundbreaking ceremony was held at the corner of Randolph Street and Michigan Avenue on July 27, 1892. Dr. Emil G. Hirsch, a prominent rabbi and Library Board president, proclaimed, "We have for years been like the ancient people of Egypt, wandering about in search of a home. At last we have reached the promised land and here we intend to remain. As the sun's heat is oppressive, I will not detain you further. I now take the first shovel of earth and cast it into the wagon." He then emptied his shovel into a nearby wagon. Others followed suit. The dirt from the excavation site was hauled to the Art Institute site where it was used for landfill.

Above: In 1891, the library board selected Shepley Rutan
and Coolidge's entry as the winning design in the competition for
the new library building.

Left: Centering for the construction of the library's exterior arches.

Below: In March 1894, the exterior granite and limestone wall began to resemble the shape of the architects' design.

Five years later, after several construction delays, the spectacular, neo-classical granite and limestone "palace" called the Chicago Public Library was finally completed. During the first week of October 1897, the people of Chicago marveled at the sparkling building that housed an inspired, marvelous library and a serenely beautiful Grand Army of the Republic War Memorial.

The Chicago Sunday Tribune said: "While its decorative splendor is surpassed by other notable libraries, particularly the new structures in Washington and Boston, its tastefulness and fitness leave little to be desired." Ten thousand Chicagoans a day flocked to see the elegant structure with its two dazzling stained-glass domes; white marble stairways and walls decorated with shimmering mother-of-pearl and colored glass mosaics; green marble war memorial rooms containing the names of important battles; and beautiful coffered ceilings.

The Washington Street staircase is dazzling in white Carrara marble and bejeweled Cosmati work.

One week later, on October 9, a gala celebration was held for nearly 3,000 guests, a "who's who" of Chicago society. At the opening, the Chicago Orchestra played the intermezzo from Pietro Mascagni's *Cavallieria Rusticana,* composed just six years before. The music accompanying the dedication foreshadowed what would be the mission of the Chicago Cultural Center nearly a century later — to support new and innovative arts.

This building is as solid as its great mass suggests. It took nearly a year for 70 men to drive 2,357 wooden piles 75 feet to the hardpan clay below Michigan Avenue's sandy soil. The design, by engineer William Sooy Smith, was so stable that there has been no noticeable settlement of the building in more than 100 years.

Left: To coincide with the dedication of the city's new library
in October 1897, the Chicago Sunday Tribune printed a supplement
detailing the library's artistic features.

Right: The July 6, 1893 edition of Engineering News
included a sketch of the successful foundation piles used in the
construction of the new library building.

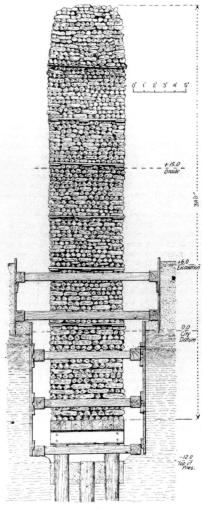

Sketch of Test Load for Foundation Piles; Chicago Public Library.

RAILROAD CARS SUPPLIED THE COAL THAT FED THE MASSIVE

BOILERS

IN THE BASEMENT.

TODAY HEAT AND HOT WATER ARE SUPPLIED BY THE PITTSFIELD BUILDING

ACROSS THE STREET.

NEWSPAPER
STANDS

ON THE RANDOLPH STREET SIDE OF THE LIBRARY ALLOWED CHICAGOANS
TO READ THE LATEST EDITIONS OF THE DAILY PAPERS

BEFORE HOME DELIVERY SERVICES
WERE WIDESPREAD.

HIGHLIGHTS OF THE BUILDING

The exterior.

The structure was originally built in the shape of a blunt-ended U. It measures 352 feet north to south, 134 feet east to west, and 90 feet from the sidewalk to the balustrade. The three-foot-thick walls are made of fine grade Bedford (Indiana) limestone on a granite base. From the outside the building appears to be three stories but inside it is actually five stories.

The interior.

The north and south sides of the building have different architectural elements. Entering from Randolph Street, the north side, the architecture is Greek-inspired with strong angular structures and military-influenced decorations. The three doorways share a massive porch with Doric columns set in pairs.

From the curving marble staircase an outdoor garden and sculpture can be viewed. At the top of the stairway is the 45-foot by 50-foot Grand Army of the Republic (G.A.R.) Rotunda. The ceiling is embossed with plaster carvings of swords, shields, helmets, and flags. This ornamental heraldry serves to remind viewers of the loss that comes with war.

The 40-foot-diameter stained-glass dome in shades of tan, beige, and ochre is now lighted electrically. It was originally illuminated by sunlight. The stained glass was made by Healy & Millet of Chicago. It is held in place by cast-iron ribbing, manufactured by the Winslow Brothers of Chicago. A floor inset with glass blocks originally provided natural light from the dome to the first floor below.

Right: Chicago art glass manufacturers, Healy & Millet, used jewel
cut glass and botanical motifs in the G.A.R. Rotunda.

The immense G.A.R. Memorial Hall is just beyond the Rotunda. It measures 53-feet long, 96-feet wide, and 33-feet high. Leased to the Grand Army Hall and Memorial Association between 1898 and 1948, it was a meeting place for members of the G.A.R. Today, the collection of Civil War artifacts once displayed there is now preserved at the Harold Washington Library Center. It is used for ceremonial and artistic purposes, including weddings.

This room is a somber and richly decorated memorial to the soldiers of the Civil War. The sedate Vermont (Verdé) marble walls bear the names of 30 Civil War battles including: Shilo, Antietam, Gettysburg, Cedar Creek, Ft. Sumter. The coffered ceilings are encrusted with dragons, fruit, stars, and other designs. Adjacent to Memorial Hall is the Claudia Cassidy Theater, originally a flat-floored G.A.R. meeting room.

Left: Detail of doorway in Memorial Hall of G.A.R. rooms

Right: The G.A.R. Memorial Hall was once furnished with bronze-footed cases filled with artifacts from the Civil War.

FORT SUMTER · PEA RIDGE
PORT ROYAL MONITOR AND MERRIMAC
FORT DONELSON SHILOH

Entering from Washington Street, the south side, the architecture is Roman-inspired. This entrance has Roman arches and exuberant ornamentation. There are three pairs of glass doors with decorative elements. A 34-foot-long elliptical arch of white marble, decorated with glass tesserae, sparkles with the names of great thinkers of the past, including Cicero, Plato, and Livy. The lobby (45 feet deep and 53 feet wide) is decorated in rare marbles. The white marble is Italian Carrara, from the same source as the marble used by Michelangelo for his sculpture. The dark green marble is Irish Connemara. Fine hardwoods, stained glass, and polished bronze are also used lavishly throughout.

The Cosmati work throughout the interior is a technique in which marble is inlaid with a variety of materials, including lustrous Favrile glass, colored stone, mother-of-pearl, gold leaf, and mosaic. This technique makes walls appear jewel-like. Due to Chicago's sooty air, the choice of glass and marble was practical as well as aesthetic because these materials last indefinitely and can be easily cleaned.

The grand staircase of white Carrara contains mosaics designed by Robert C. Spencer, Jr. of Shepley Rutan and Coolidge. The mosaics were executed in the Tiffany Studios in New York by J.A. Holzer. Above the third floor the staircase is decorated with less elaborate Italian and American marbles and mosaics.

Left: After 100 years, the mosaics in the Washington Street lobby
continue to dazzle visitors with their vibrant colors.

Right: Mother-of-pearl, Favrile glass, and gold leaf are assembled in intricate
patterns in the building's numerous examples of Cosmati work.

ON THE THIRD FLOOR THE STAIRCASE OPENS INTO THE ELEGANT

PRESTON BRADLEY HALL,

WHICH SPANS THE WIDTH OF THE BUILDING.

ORIGINALLY, THIS WAS THE GENERAL DELIVERY ROOM

WHERE PEOPLE RECEIVED THE BOOKS THEY REQUESTED.

The world's largest Tiffany dome is a stunning backdrop for the many concerts, weddings and other special events hosted in Preston Bradley Hall today.

The magnificent translucent dome, 38 feet in diameter and made of Tiffany Favrile glass, is cut in the shape of fish scales. At the top of the dome are the signs of the zodiac. Now lighted electrically, it was originally illuminated by sunlight. At the base of the dome is a quotation from the British author Joseph Addison. The dome glass, lighting fixtures, wall sconces and chandeliers were made by the Tiffany Glass and Decorating Company of New York. The supporting frame was constructed by the Chicago Ornamental Iron Company. On the east and west sides of the hall are quotations in Greek, Chinese, Arabic, Egyptian hieroglyphics, Hebrew, Italian, German, French, Latin, and Spanish. Black ornamented boxes in the corners of the room were once elevators used for book delivery.

Left: Louis Comfort Tiffany's mosaics in Preston Bradley Hall were inspired by printer's marks that were well known by Chicago's bibliophiles.

Right: Detail of the art glass dome designed by the Tiffany Glass and Decorating Company of New York.

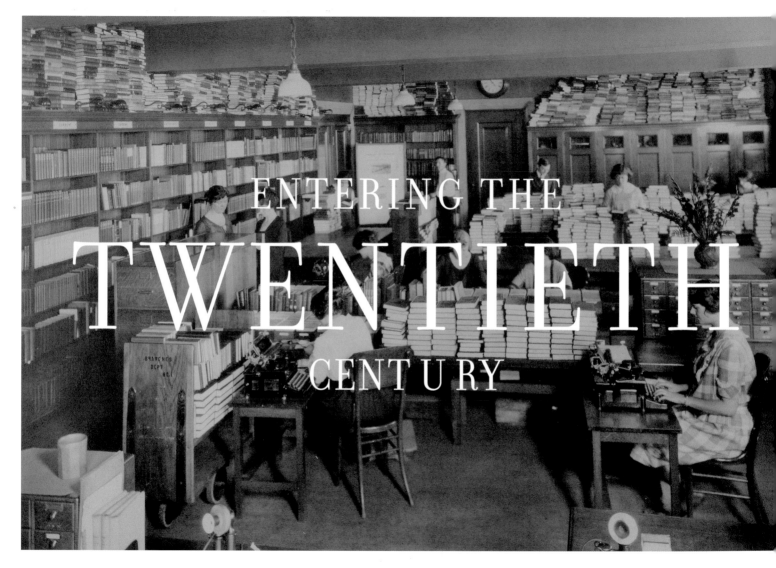

ENTERING THE TWENTIETH CENTURY

Circulation desk in Delivery Room, c. 1945

By 1915 cultural programming was a regular feature at the library. By the mid-1920s the library began to outgrow its space. As early as the 1930s the inadequate space at the library became a topic of public discussion. Between the 1930s and 1970s the scope of the library's offerings continued to expand; it was clearly overcrowded.

EVEN AS EARLY AS THE 1920S, THE CHICAGO

PUBLIC LIBRARY HAD ALREADY ESTABLISHED ITSELF AS A

LANDMARK

IN THE HEARTS OF CHICAGOANS.

DO YOU KNOW THIS BUILDING? IT'S YOURS.

A replica of the building was mounted on a car and used as a parade float in the '20s.

A **1967** ARCHITECTURAL SURVEY CONDUCTED BY CHICAGO ARCHITECTS
HOLABIRD AND ROOT CONFIRMED THAT ALTHOUGH THE BUILDING WAS STILL

STRUCTURALLY SOUND,

THE MECHANICAL, ELECTRICAL AND COMMUNICATION SYSTEMS WERE

OBSOLETE.

SOME CHANGES WERE NECESSARY.

This telephone operating cabinet was once regarded as one of the examples of the library's cutting-edge technology.

The library building is saved.

A design competition for the renovation of the Chicago Public Library was held in 1970. Two architectural firms from Madison, Wisconsin shared the prize for the winning design, estimating that the project would cost a prohibitive $28 million. Soon the library became the center of a spirited public debate. City officials were challenged to provide Chicagoans with a cost-effective, updated public library and some suggested that the building be demolished. Preservationists wanted to save it, both for its magnificent beauty and as a monument to the past.

During the early 1970s, the demolition of old buildings in the name of progress and modernization was a common response to the aging of American cities. Chicago was no exception and the Chicago Public Library building seemed doomed to share the fate of the recently demolished Board of Trade building.

On February 7, 1972, Mayor Richard J. Daley formed a special six-man committee to consider the building's future. Four days later, in a rare public comment, Eleanor "Sis" Daley, the Mayor's wife, was quoted in the Chicago press as saying, "I am for restoring and keeping all the beautiful buildings." Within three weeks, the Mayor's committee announced that the building would be saved.

Preservationists cheered. The Chicago Public Library would be moved to a new site. Not only would one of Chicago's most beautiful buildings be saved, but this decision would help to save other historic treasures in the future. In another important move Senator Adlai Stevenson III (D. Illinois) succeeded in having the building placed on the National Register of Historic Places because it was "a precious public resource." This designation, granted in 1972, would also protect it from future demolition.

The library is renovated: 1974 – 1977

Approximately half of the library's books and periodicals had been moved to another location by 1974. Consequently, the library's collection was then housed in two facilities. That same year, the firm of Holabird and Root was selected as the architects for a much-needed building renovation. The architects viewed the structure as an historic treasure and their sensitive design kept the exterior and most of its decorative features intact and unchanged.

When the project was completed three years later, Holabird and Root were lauded for their skillful work — modernizing an outdated structure while preserving its historic integrity.

What did the architects do?

During the renovation, old space was put to new use. Along Garland Court, on the west side of the structure, a long, gently sloping ramp was constructed to provide easy access between several floors and the building's north and south sections. The ramp also enclosed the original U-shape of the building, allowing for a lovely sculpture garden. A major exhibition space was created out of former stack-filled library rooms and the G.A.R. meeting room became a formal theater seating 294 people. In addition, the glorious Tiffany-domed book delivery room gained new life as the Preston Bradley Hall, providing a dazzling setting for functions from concerts to luncheons. In 1976, The Commission on Chicago Historical and Architectural Landmarks granted the building status as a Chicago Landmark.

Martin Puryear installation in the fourth floor exhibit hall, formerly the reference room.

The rise of the Chicago
Cultural Center.

Imaginative support by the Chicago City Council and succeeding mayoral administrations during the 1970s and 1980s fostered the evolution of the Chicago Public Library Cultural Center. In 1976, during the administration of Mayor Michael Bilandic, the Chicago Council on Fine Arts was established to publicly support individual artists and arts organizations. In 1977, the building became known as The Chicago Public Library Cultural Center. Mayor Jane Byrne moved the funding for programs and staff from the library to the Chicago Council on Fine Arts in 1981. In 1984, Mayor Harold Washington's administration created the Chicago Department of Cultural Affairs to provide free arts and cultural services to all Chicagoans, and the programming role became part of the new department.

In 1986, Mayor Richard M. Daley announced a design competition for a new library that would be located on West Congress Boulevard. In 1989 Mayor Daley appointed Lois Weisberg as Commissioner of the Chicago Department of Cultural Affairs. In 1991, the new Harold Washington Library Center was dedicated. Soon after, Mayor

Preston Bradley Hall, with its luminous Tiffany Mosaics, is now the site of numerous free concerts.

Daley decided that the venerable building on Michigan Avenue should become a free museum and cultural center. Created by visionaries who believed that the arts should be free to the public and part of their daily experience, the Chicago Cultural Center evolved as a national model. Referring to its genesis, Commissioner Weisberg said, "It was a dream come true for those who love the arts and view them as an essential public service that should be free and accessible to everyone. There is no place like it in the country." To this day, Commissioner Weisberg holds the same position.

Thanks to the efforts of Congressman Sidney R. Yates (D. Illinois), the Chicago Cultural Center received $2 million from the federal government for a partial renovation, completed in 1994. That same year, the Sidney R. Yates Gallery, a beautiful exhibition space, was dedicated. The momentum continued and the Chicago Cultural Center soon boasted a Studio Theater, Dance Studio, Café, Shop and three more galleries. Today, the Museum of Broadcast Communications is another popular attraction and Renaissance Court, operated by the Chicago Department on Aging, serves an important population.

Right: During the 1980s, the Sidney R. Yates Gallery was
restored to its original splendor, and now serves as one of the premier
exhibition spaces within the Chicago Cultural Center.

**The Chicago Cultural
Center today.**

The Chicago Cultural Center attracts thousands of visitors each year — people of all ages and nationalities, residents and tourists — who experience the hundreds of regularly scheduled public events offered free of charge. It is known for exhibitions, music, drama and dance; for lectures, demonstrations and workshops; screenings and plays; and concerts and discussions. The Chicago Cultural Center is a special place, a People's Palace, where everyone who enters its grand lobbies has a unique opportunity to be entertained, enlightened, and enriched.

Glossary.

arch
a curved structure, as of masonry, that supports the weight of material over an open space, as in a doorway, window or bridge

coffered
ornamented with recessed panels that form a continuous pattern

Cosmati
technique in which marble is inlaid with a variety of materials, including lustrous Favrile glass, colored stone, mother-of-pearl, gold leaf, and mosaic

dome
a hemispherical roof form

Doric column
one of the five Classical orders, it consists of a plain, narrow, rounded capital and a fluted shaft that does not rest on a base

Favrile
a trademark registered by the Tiffany Glass & Decorating Co. in 1894 for its blown glass, "a composition of various colored glasses, worked together while hot"

inlaid
set in pieces into a surface of another material so as to form a smooth surface

Ionic column
one of the five Classical orders, characterized by a fluted shaft and a capital of large scrolled volutes

molding
any continuous projecting or inset architectural member with a contoured profile

mosaic
a surface decoration created by small pieces of cemented glass, stone, or tile laid in the form of patterns or representational pictures

mother-of-pearl
the hard, pearly internal layer of certain marine shells, as of the pearl oyster, abalone, etc. used in the arts

neo-Classical
the readaptation and reuse of the principles of Greek and Roman architecture, including the concepts of logical construction and truth to materials

tesserae
small cubes of glass, stone, or marble used in mosaic

Photography credits.

[Detail Healy & Millet dome]
Hedrich-Blessing, photographers
Courtesy of Department of
Cultural Affairs

[GAR Rotunda]
Hedrich-Blessing, photographers
Courtesy of Department of
Cultural Affairs

Hedrich-Blessing, photographers
Courtesy of Department of
Cultural Affairs

[Memorial Hall]
Hedrich-Blessing, photographers
Courtesy of Department of
Cultural Affairs

[Mosaic Washington Street
Lobby]
Hedrich-Blessing, photographers
Courtesy of Department of
Cultural Affairs

[Detail of cosmati work]
Hedrich-Blessing, photographers
Courtesy of Department of
Cultural Affairs

[Preston Bradley Hall looking
east]
Hedrich-Blessing, photographers
Courtesy of Department of
Cultural Affairs

[Detail of mosaic printer's mark]
Hedrich-Blessing, photographers
Courtesy of Department of
Cultural Affairs

[Tiffany dome, PBH]
Hedrich-Blessing, photographers
Courtesy of Department of
Cultural Affairs

[Bindery Department]
Courtesy of Special Collections
and Preservation Division,
Chicago Public Library

[Circulation desk]
Courtesy of Special Collections
and Preservation Division,
Chicago Public Library

[Do You Know This Building?]
Courtesy of Special Collections
and Preservation Division,
Chicago Public Library

[Telephone operator]
Courtesy of Special Collections
and Preservation Division,
Chicago Public Library

[Martin Puryear installation]
Courtesy of Department of
Cultural Affairs

[PBH with reflection in grand
piano]
Hedrich-Blessing, photographers
Courtesy of Department of
Cultural Affairs

[Sidney Yates Gallery]
Hedrich-Blessing, photographers
Courtesy of Department of
Cultural Affairs

[Washington Street staircase,
entrance to PBH]
Hedrich-Blessing, photographers
Courtesy of Department of
Cultural Affairs